SUPER SPORTS STORIES

# KAREEM'S AMAZING KARATE KICK

by Blake Hoena

illustrated by Christos Skaltsas

## Tools for Parents & Teachers

Grasshopper Books enhance imagination and introduce the earliest readers to fiction with fun storylines and illustrations. The easy-to-read text supports early reading experiences with repetitive sentence patterns and sight words.

### Before Reading

- Discuss the cover illustration. What do readers see?
- Look at the glossary together. Discuss the words.

### Read the Book

- Read the book to the child, or have him or her read independently.
- "Walk" through the book and look at the illustrations. Who is the main character? What is happening in the story?

### After Reading

- Prompt the child to think more. Ask: Kareem feels confident when he breaks a board in his karate lesson. What helps you feel confident?

Grasshopper Books are published by Jump!
5357 Penn Avenue South
Minneapolis, MN 55419
www.jumplibrary.com



Library of Congress Cataloging-in-Publication Data

Names: Hoena, B. A., author. | Skaltsas, Christos, illustrator.
Title: Kareem's amazing karate kick / by Blake Hoena; illustrated by Christos Skaltsas.
Description: Minneapolis, MN: Jump!, Inc., [2024]
Series: Super sports stories | Includes index.
Audience: Ages 7-10.
Identifiers: LCCN 2022049556 (print)
LCCN 2022049557 (ebook)
ISBN 9798885243889 (hardcover)
ISBN 9798885243896 (paperback)
ISBN 9798885243902 (ebook)
Subjects: CYAC: Self-Confidence–Fiction. | Karate–Fiction.
LCGFT: Sports fiction. | Readers (Publications)
Classification: LCC PZ7.H67127 Kar 2024 (print)
LCC PZ7.H67127 (ebook)
DDC [Fic] –dc23
LC record available at https://lccn.loc.gov/2022049556
LC ebook record available at https://lccn.loc.gov/2022049557

Editor: Eliza Leahy
Direction and Layout: Anna Peterson
Illustrator: Christos Skaltsas

Printed in the United States of America at
Corporate Graphics in North Mankato, Minnesota.

## Table of Contents



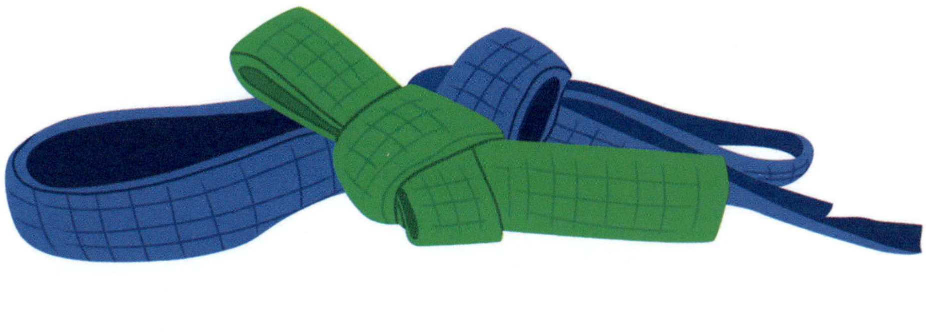

# Confidence Boost

Kareem and his friend Ryan meet outside their dojo.

"Hey! How was school today?" Ryan asks.

"It was rough," Kareem replies. "I failed a quiz."

Before their karate lesson, they both bow and whisper, “Osu.” This is a sign of respect.

“Bummer about the quiz,” Ryan says. “Maybe you will feel better after our lesson.”

“My confidence sure could use a boost,” Kareem says.

Just then, Sensei Craig calls out, “Line up!”

The students get in line according to their belt color.

"At the end of class, we will break boards," Sensei Craig announces. "It's a great way to build confidence in your skills."

The other students are excited. But Kareem isn't. *Not sure I'm up for that after my rough day,* he thinks.

After stretches and warm-ups, the students work on blocking drills.

Kareem and Ryan work together. Kareem steps forward to throw a punch. Ryan does an upward block.

"Good form, Ryan," Sensei Craig says.

Ryan throws a punch. Kareem attempts a side block.

"Try not to lower your elbow too much, Kareem," Sensei Craig says.

*I'm trying*, Kareem thinks.

The students continue blocking drills. Toward the end of class, Sensei Craig calls, “Line up!”

Everyone quickly gets back in their place.

“Are you ready to break a board?” Ryan whispers to Kareem.

“I don’t know,” Kareem replies. “I haven’t tried it before.”

“It is time to break boards! Remember to stay focused. Have confidence,” Sensei Craig tells his students.

When it is Ryan’s turn, he punches and shouts, “Hi-yah!”

The board snaps in two.

Then, it is Kareem's turn.

*Stay focused*, he thinks. *Be confident.*

He quickly lifts his back leg and kicks forward.

*CRACK!* The board snaps in half.

*I did it!* Kareem thinks.

“Good job, Kareem!” Sensei Craig says.

Kareem and Ryan high-five.

“How are you feeling now?” Ryan asks.

“Much better!” Kareem says. “In fact, I feel like I can ace my test tomorrow.”

# Let's Review!

Kareem is a green belt. What does each belt color mean in karate? Take a look!

A beginner.

A beginner who has learned basic blocks and strikes.

A beginner who is learning more advanced moves.

An intermediate student who is learning combat moves.

An intermediate student who is learning to spar.

An intermediate student who is learning more advanced combat skills.

An advanced student who might begin teaching other students.

An advanced student who is mastering complex skills.

An advanced student who is extremely skilled and knowledgeable.

## Karate Equipment

Kareem wears a karate uniform called a gi. What are the parts of a gi? Take a look!

## To Learn More

**Finding more information is as easy as 1, 2, 3.**

1. Go to www.factsurfer.com
2. Enter "**Kareem'samazingkaratekick**" into the search box.
3. Choose your book to see a list of websites.

# Glossary

**blocking:** Making an opponent's movements difficult.

**boost:** Something that cheers you up or makes you feel better.

**confidence:** A belief that you have the necessary ability to succeed.

**dojo:** A place where people practice martial arts.

**drills:** Exercises done regularly to practice and perfect skills.

**focused:** Concentrated on something or somebody.

**form:** A certain way of doing something.

**osu:** A word commonly spoken when entering a dojo, greeting a teacher, or before sparring to show respect.

**sensei:** A martial arts instructor.

**skills:** Abilities to do things well.

**warm-ups:** A set of exercises done in order to get ready for a performance or competition.

# Index